WRITING RE-CREATIVELY

A Spiritual Quest for Women

GAIL RANADIVE

The Columbine Press
Mt. Vernon, Virginia

Writing Re-Creatively:
A Spiritual Quest for Women

The author wishes to express her gratitude to the Unitarian Universalist
Women's Federation for a 1991 Feminist Theology Award that helped
make this book possible.

Special thanks to Stacy Tuthill, Carolyn Cottom, and Betty Jo Middleton
for their editorial advice and assistance.

Some of these poems have appeared in the following publications:
American Literary, *Earth's Daughters*, *Folio*, *Friendly Woman*.

Also by Gail Ranadive:
If You'd Been Born In India, Albert Whitman & Co., 1973.

"William Ellery Channing," "Susan B. Anthony," "Olympia Brown,"
"Mark Morrison-Reed" in *Unitarian Universalism in the Home*, 1982.

Cover drawing by Gail Ranadive
Typography by Barbara Shaw
Photo by Cassie Arnold

ISBN 0-9632859-0-4
Library of Congress Catalog Card # 92-81603

The Columbine Press
P.O. Box 153
Mt. Vernon, VA 22121-0153

For, of, and by
the feminine
arising among us.

To
Peggy,

with warm wishes,
Gail Paradine
August '92

CONTENTS

THIS BOOK IS A SLIM VOLUME FOR A REASON. It grew out of a workshop I created for my M.F.A. internship. And, as I've led several versions of it over the last five years, it has evolved to the point where I could write many pages on each topic. In fact, each topic could become a workshop in itself, and perhaps, one day, will. But not now. The point here is not for me to go on and on with my words, my insights, my ideas and experiences, but to evoke yours. I do not mean to suggest that what is true for me is also necessarily true for you; rather, I challenge you to name your own truth. My discussion of an issue is not to be taken as a final, authoritative word, but as a starting point for your own thinking, or re-thinking.

I will briefly discuss a topic I have researched, then rephrase it as a writing exercise. You will find samples of other women's writings on the topic in the Appendix, should you choose to refer to it.

Next, you are invited to write for eight to ten minutes on the topic. This limited concentration of time will prevent you from censoring what wants to come out! (The facilitator of the workshop may decide to give one minute and "finish up" reminders.)

Then, if you are doing this workshop in a group, I suggest you go around and give everyone a chance to read what they have written. This works best if no one is allowed to comment on what's been written. Everyone is free to pass, but encouraged not to; each person has a piece of our collective story. You will each hear yourself and others name what you didn't know you knew. And that is the whole point.

There are thirty writing exercises to work with. I see them grouped in threes that chronologically work off one another and move forward. They can also be used in sets of twos, depending on the size of the group and the length of time you have set aside to work on this together. The larger the group, the more time will be needed to hear everyone's work. You may even decide to do only one exercise per session, then discuss your insights and ideas after you've read what you've written without comment. The point is to do what works best for you. Your group will evolve its own sense of bonding and its own set of dynamics. You may even come up with additional writing exercises on a topic that has opened up issues for you as reflected in your writing. (I have enclosed my working bibliography for your additional reading.)

It is time to begin: to name, honor, and value ourselves as women. Our experience of the world is different from men's, beginning in early childhood. Yet the world we live in has been named, defined, and constructed from the male perspective, as if it were universal. It isn't. It is time to stop fitting ourselves sideways into history, psychology, sociology, spirituality, and philosophy as conceived of, for, and by men. We need to balance the male world-view that threatens to destroy the planet environmentally, economically, militarily. But in order to do that, we must first recreate the images, symbols, and metaphors of our own lives, as women.

The essays and exercises are headed with "re" words to indicate the process of restoration to a previous condition. We are not creating something out of nothing. Rather, we will write in order to tap into what's already within us, hidden, hibernating, waiting to be reawakened and given voice.

One

RETREAT TO A SAFE PLACE

Retreat: a quiet, private, secure place; refuge
a period of seclusion or solitude

AS YOU COME TOGETHER FOR THE FIRST TIME, or as
you begin this work alone, find a way to make the space
sacred. Perhaps you'll choose to light a candle as a symbol of
the living presence that is both within and beyond our own
being. It can also be a way to focus, to center yourself in the
moment. Our word for *focus* comes from the Latin word for
fireplace, the hearth at the center of the home. And the
sacred fire was brought to the home from the temple of
Vesta, the Greeks' Hestia, Goddess of the Hearth who
personifies the archetype of the Self.

Begin by introducing yourself. Knowing that everything
written and read in this space will remain here, how will you
identify yourself?

You might choose to follow a standard I.D. format, giving
your name, occupation, size, age, colorings, etc., perhaps
adding some things you'd like to see included on it, such as
vocation, parental status, etc.

In western cultures, we often choose to identify ourselves
through what we do, and give our qualifications to authorize
our work. For instance, the biographical note at the back of
this book outlines my credentials for creating this course.

In many eastern cultures, one is often identified through
one's relationship within a family. For instance, it has been
the custom in India for the son's new wife to change her last
name to his, her middle name to his first name, and her first
name to whatever new name her in-laws choose for her. My
in-laws call me "Nilakshi," girl with the blue eyes. But my

husband's younger brother always and only calls me "Vahini," sister-in-law.

For eight to ten minutes, identify, describe, introduce ourself, on paper. What do you want the group to know about you? Or, what do you want to say about yourself to yourself? (For sample writings, see the Appendix, page 65.)

Read aloud what you have written. Remember, do not interrupt yourself or anyone else with comments, explanations, reactions. Simply listen to what has come up and out through the hand onto the page.

Two

RECONSIDER WHO YOU REALLY ARE

> *Reconsider: to consider (deliberate upon, examine; to
> think or dream; to believe or judge) again*

FILLING OUT THE CONVENTIONAL I.D. FORM requires
using the analytic side of the brain: the side that separates
the whole picture into its constituent parts.

But we have another side to our brain: the side that
perceives analogically. This is the side that comprehends
complex wholes instantly and intuitively. By imagining
similarities between dissimilar things, this part of the brain
sees more than what literally meets the eye.

My analytical identity deals with my teaching experience,
my writing situation, and my poetry publication. But while I
was developing the outer identity, I was inwardly living in
the image of a turtle. Let me explain. For political and
personal reasons, I remained behind on the east coast for the
two years that my husband was stationed in California with
the army. All our household goods went with him. Our
house was rented out. All I had with me was what I could fit
in the trunk of a my ten-year-old car. I rented space in a
friend's home, I house-sat for a church member, I partici-
pated in a fellowship and a writing residency—all to stay on
the east coast and begin my teaching and writing career. I
felt (and lived) like a turtle: plodding slowly forward, not
daring to look back. A turtle sees only what's right in front
of its eyes at each moment: blades of grass, a red mushroom,
obstacles to go around or over top of. Survival is the main
goal. There's not much of a perspective from that angle: no
eagle-eye view of the whole picture. But by accepting the
image of the turtle for the time being, I intuitively knew I,
too, could survive.

For eight to ten minutes, explore an image from nature, animal, vegetable, or mineral, that best describes who you are, at this time in your life, here and now. (For sample writings, see the Appendix, page 66.)

Read aloud what you have written.

Three

RE-ENTER THAT OTHER COUNTRY

Re-entry: entering a second or subsequent time

AS WE ARE ALL AWARE, our present world has come to prefer, value, and rely upon the side of the brain that deals with analytic thinking. This was not necessarily always the case. In *The Underside of History*, Elise Boulding claims there is strong evidence to suggest that our forbears used both sides of the brain equally. They were ambidextrous until the Paleolithic period, when they shifted to right-handedness as hunters. At that time, the left hand, and the side of the brain that controlled it, became less used and increasingly devalued. A dualism based on the use of the right and left hand began to evolve:

right	*left*
strong	weak
day	night
male	female
life	death
good	evil
high	low
sacred	profane

When this dualism became irreversible, Boulding points out, the image of women (as non-hunters? as still ambidextrous?) became permanently fixed on the "negative" side of the listing. And male superiority and dominance began in earnest.

In order to retrieve what got lost while language was developing out of the analytic side of the brain, we must re-enter what feminist literary critic Helene Cixous calls "that other limitless country." It is that unconscious place where the repressed (women? fairies?) has "managed to survive."

For eight to ten minutes, write about that which can not, or has not, been named. Is there something you sense vaguely, below the level of articulation, something you *act* out of? (For a sample writing, see the Appendix, page 67.)

Read aloud what you have written.

Four

RECOVER YOUR FAVORITE TREE

Recover: to get back; regain

AS WOMEN IN A MALE DOMINATED CULTURE, we
know in our bones that the language we speak is of, for, and
by our fathers, brothers, husbands, lovers, sons. We know
this when we become frustrated, angry, or invisible when
the men we love can't hear/don't grasp what we are trying to
say. And so, more often than not, we give up, and continue
to fit ourselves into the images, symbols, metaphors, and
myths of our male oriented culture that define us only in
relationship to the male "norm."

But in doing so, we do violence to who we ourselves are.
Living in the formlessness that exists below the level of
language, we have no words to shape into stories that name
who we are, and therefore cannot make meaning out of our
life experiences. We remain in the limitless country, silent
and silenced.

In her book *Stealing the Language*, Alicia Ostriker tells us
that women poets are continually trying to make the
language say what they need it to say. Is this possible? By
going back to the roots of words, we often find they began
as visual images. For example, a daisy is a day's eye; disaster
means to be separated from the stars. Before becoming fixed,
each word was a figurative image that activated the analogic
part of the brain.

For eight to ten minutes, write about a TREE. What kind of
tree comes to mind? Is it a specific tree, perhaps one out of
your childhood? What is your relationship to it? What does
it symbolize for you? Does it want to become a metaphor?

9

For what? Let the TREE take you where IT wants to go. (For sample writings, see the Appendix, page 68.)

(I chose the word tree here because, while I was studying with one of his original pupils in Europe, I learned that Carl Jung found that many of his female analysands pictured their psychological/spiritual selves as trees.)

Read aloud what you have written.

Five

RESURRECT THE SERPENT

> *Resurrect: to bring back to life; to bring back into*
> *practice, notice, or use*

IMAGES THAT LIE DEEP WITHIN OUR PSYCHES cannot
be dealt with on a rational level, i.e., out of the analytical
part of the brain. As Nelle Morton notes in *The Journey is
Home*, an image is not merely a mental picture; it is a
dynamic through which both an individual and the body
politic communicate. Images shape life-styles and values,
one's sense of self and of structures of power. They take on a
life of their own, beyond our conscious control.

Take, for instance, the image of the serpent. No matter
how hard I try, I cannot seem to overcome my aversion to
snakes, no doubt left over from my Protestant upbringing.
Yet I recall the sterling silver caduceus on the charm bracelet
I wore as an off-duty student nurse; its serpent was a symbol
of health and healing. Today, I also know that the serpent
was once associated with the goddess and the feminine
power of life. The shedding of the serpent's skin and the
monthly shedding of the lining of a woman's womb both
symbolize renewal. I know this intellectually. But, when I
come across newly emerged water snakes in the wild life
sanctuary I frequent, I have to use every ounce of will power
to stand my ground, and not run in the other direction!

Can we retrieve the images that the patriarchy has
coopted and often actually turned against us women?
Barbara G. Walker's *The Woman's Dictionary of Symbols and
Sacred Objects* begins this process. In one of her twenty-
seven entries on the serpent, she reveals that the serpent/hair
of Medusa symbolized menstrual mysteries, the knowledge

of which could turn men to stone. The blood of the be-
headed Medusa gave birth to Pegasus, the winged horse of
poetic inspiration. It is only through a poetic revision
(seeing again) of the images that we can begin to disrupt the
subliminal hold they have over us.

*For eight to ten minutes, write about the serpent; let the
image lead your words to where they want to go.* (For a sample
writing, see the Appendix, page 69.)

Read aloud what you have written.

REVIEW A BIBLICAL IMAGE

*Review: to look over or study again; to examine with an
eye to criticism or correction; to reconsider*

IN *MYTHS TO LIVE BY*, Joseph Campbell proposes that all
the great religions and mythologies of the world are actually
poems that are to be interpreted figuratively rather than
literally. Reading his book was a turning point in my life. I
had been struggling to understand how and why I kept
finding stories that paralleled my Christian heritage in the
books I brought back from India for my children. In them
were virgin births, savior figures walking on water, great
floods, etc. Clearly there was something deep within the
human psyche that transcended particular cultures. But
why?

Campbell outlines four reasons for myths and religions in
the human experience. First, there's the cosmological
function: to define a people's place in the universe. Second,
the sociological function of myth defines the individual's
place within the culture into which one's been born. Next
comes the psychological function: to guide a person through
all the stages of a useful life. And finally, there is a spiritual
dimension to myths: to give one an actual experience of the
transcendent mystery, whatever one chooses to call it.

Unpleasant things happen when people accept their
religious stories as literally true, and everyone else's as false,
pagan, heretical, heathen, or misguided. But what happens if
we re-read our culture's stories as poems, from the analogic
part of the brain?

The good news about figurative language is this: it is
dynamic, open-ended, growing, changeable. There are as

many interpretations of a poem as there are readers. Does it really matter what the poet meant? Often the ambiguous words and images in the poem were used so that the reader might grasp what's going on in her or his own life at that moment.

For eight to ten minutes, recall a Biblical image, metaphor, parable, or story and use it in a way that is new for you. (For a sample writing, see the Appendix, page 70.)

Read aloud what you have written.

Seven

REVIVE YOUR EARLIER SELF

> *Revive: to bring or come back to life or consciousness; to impart or regain vigor or spirit*

FOR THE NEXT THREE SESSIONS, we'll consider Campbell's concept of the sociological function of myth. He reminds us that we human beings are born some twelve years too soon. Unlike our animal counterparts, we cannot survive on our own for many years after our birth. Therefore, we are born into families, as a sort of second womb.

Those early years can be filled with wonder as we acquire the fundamentals of human culture. Every day becomes an adventure as we learn and experience and grow physically, psychologically, and intellectually. These are truly magical years!

Yet two recent studies commissioned by the American Association of University Women report on a disturbing phenomenon revealed in their research: somewhere around the age of eleven, girls seem to come up against a wall that blocks their further learning and unfolding. Why? The research shows that between elementary and middle school, girls become aware of the dichotomy between what their parents and teachers encourage them to do and be and what society will actually allow them to be and do in their lives. At this point, girls begin to withdraw and internalize that they are not as good, as smart, as capable as their brothers. This process reinforces itself. As a girl stops speaking up in class, or claims that she doesn't know the answer (which she did know a year earlier), she is called on less and less, and becomes more and more invisible. Her self esteem plummets; depression sets in, eating disorders develop. Whereas adolescence is a time when boys open up to the possibilities life offers, for girls it can become a time of closing down, in order to fit into the limited role society demands of females: sugar and spice and everything nice—quiet, compliant, or, as my mother remembers me as a child: the perfect little lady.

For eight to ten minutes, try to recapture, with words, the person you were becoming before you were socialized to be otherwise. (For sample writings, see the Appendix, page 71.)

Read aloud what you have written.

Eight

REFLECT ON A CHILDHOOD RITUAL

*Reflect: to mirror or become mirrored; to manifest as a
result of one's actions; to think or consider
seriously; to bring blame or reproach*

NOT UNLIKE OUR ANIMAL COUNTERPARTS, we
humans are imprinted by the rites, rituals, and taboos of
society through our families. Just as rituals brought order
into our personal childhoods, there is comfort in knowing
that certain things will happen at the same time in the same
place each day, such as the bedtime story. Somehow, when
there's order outside of ourselves, we can bring order to the
chaos within ourselves as well. Family rituals, even those we
detest, bring stability to our lives. We know without a doubt
what is expected of us and when, if not always why. The
explanations don't always make sense, of course: changing
underwear daily in case you get into a accident, cleaning up
your plate because people are starving in——, etc. But they
remain ingrained in our psyches, and we continue to re-
enact them in our daily lives, often unconsciously. Often
any change will bring discomfort, resistance, disorientation.

For example, I was raised to eat with a knife, fork and
spoon. But when I'm visiting my in-laws in India, I'm
expected to eat with my fingers, using only my right hand.
(The left hand is taboo. I am, naturally, left handed.) In fact,
so much in Indian culture is opposite from what I was
taught in my New England home that I wrote a children's
book in an effort to sort it all out! And I'll never forget
visiting a mosque in New Delhi and taking my shoes off.
The two Philadelphia school teachers in the tour group
looked down at my stockinged feet and exclaimed, "You
must be from Boston!" It has taken me a long time to learn

to be comfortable wearing sandals, without stockings, in public: I feel naked.

For eight to ten minutes, re-examine a rite, ritual or taboo you've carried since childhood. Do you know the rationale behind it? Does it matter? What did you pass on to your children? Why? Why not? What did you/would you change? (For a sample writing, see Appendix, page 72.)

Read aloud what you have written.

Nine

RECOUNT A FAMILY STORY

Recount: to narrate the facts or particulars of

FAMILY STORIES ARE ANOTHER METHOD by which we become socialized, humanized, civilized. The tales told to us about our kin and our place in the clan transmit family values and present us with role models to either emulate or reject. Through the stories we're told about courtship, lost fortunes, and survival, we are expected to take our place in the next generation. Do we go on to further the family ideals? Or do we become the black sheep? No matter how we finally live out our own lives, we remain connected to our family of origin, for better or for worse. We cannot divorce our family heritage.

The family name "Ranadive" means "glory of the battle-field," and reflects that my husband was born into the warrior caste of Hinduism. So it should have come as no great surprise that he got drafted into the U.S. Army (before becoming a U.S. citizen!) and enjoyed a twenty-three-year career in the military. But it was a surpise to me. Without knowing why, I found I was very uncomfortable being part of the military. In an attempt to come to terms with this, I took classes in military history and national security policy and eventually ended up doing an M.A. in Peace Studies. I worked with the campaign that lobbied the National Peace Academy bill through Congress in 1985. Yet it was seven years later that I learned that following about my mother's ancestry: Heinrich and Rachel Stief, a couple of Dutch-Baltic origin, left Europe in the early 1790's to avoid religious persecution. They were members of a devout Protestant sect that believed in simplicity of worship, communal living, and pacifism. Upon arriving in Philadelphia, they learned that, with the American Revolution impending, men were about to be required to do compulsory military service. So they emigrated to Canada, with their seven sons. I finally feel "at home!"

For eight to ten minutes, begin to reclaim a family story that helped shape you, consciously or unconsciously. (For a sample writing, see page 73.)

Read aloud what you have written.

Ten

REFINE A SEASONAL CUSTOM

Refine: to purify

ONE STEP BEYOND THE FAMILY STORIES that shape us are the folk tales (fables, legends, nursery rhymes, epics, fairy tales) we hear as children. In *Children and Books*, May Hill Arbuthnot discusses this accumulated wisdom of ordinary "folk" as an effort to understand natural events, deal with other people, and express universally experienced emotions. Folktales contain elements of older religions, historical events, rituals and superstitions. They serve as "the cement of society" by mirroring morality: good will triumph over evil.

One of the theories of the origin of folk tales holds that they are the remnants of the pagan (country folk) beliefs forced underground by the advance of Christianity. When my daughters were children, I desperately sought ways to celebrate our cultural holidays without being overtly Christian; I wanted them to value their Hindu heritage as well. Fortunately, I came across Edna Barth's series of holiday books that include *Holly, Reindeer, and Colored Lights*; *Lilies, Rabbits and Painted Eggs*; *Witches, Pumpkins, and Grinning Ghosts* in which she explained the origins of each season's symbols. What a joy to discover, for example, that the custom of decorating an evergreen tree at the winter solstice went back as far as the Druids, my Celtic ancestors. And that the word "Easter" may have come from the Anglo-Saxon pre-Christian goddess of springtime and dawn called "Eostre."

I find that I have an almost biological need to recognize and celebrate the changing of the seasons. It doesn't even matter whether there are children in the house or not. In fact, when I lived alone in a furnished, rented apartment for nine months a few years ago, the first thing I bought was not dishes, pans, or linens, but a live Christmas tree in a pot. It was August at the time, and every month I bought a glass ornament to symbolize my journey.

For eight to ten minutes, name a particular ritual custom you must carry out for a sense of connectedness to the universe. What do you feel compelled, from within, to do? (For a sample writing, see Appendix, page 74.)

Read aloud what you have written.

Eleven
RELATE A FICTIONAL LIFE

*Relate: to narrate or tell; to bring into logical
association; to interact meaningfully*

PREPARING FOR AND CARRYING OUT the annual
celebrations and traditions of the family are usually the
responsibility of the women. It is out of women's sphere of
home and hearth that have come the jokes, stories, customs,
beliefs, songs, and legends of woman's folklore, which
differs greatly from men's. In fact, women's beliefs and value
systems are so different that they often go unnoticed by the
men.

This is shown beautifully in Susan Glaspell's play *Trifles*.
An isolated farm wife has clearly murdered her husband by
knotting a rope around his neck while he slept. But the
sheriff and two other men can find no evidence to prove
this, no matter how hard they search in the house and the
barn. Meanwhile, the sheriff's wife and another woman,
brought along to fetch some clothes for the woman being
held in jail, are able to read such "trifling" details as dirty
pans under the sink, burst jars of fruit, and erratically
stitched quilt squares, and piece together the motive for the
murder. And because the men are so patronizing towards
them in the story, the women close ranks to keep their
information from the men (not difficult!) and protect the
farm wife. The short story version, which has just appeared
in the "canon" of college reading lists, is called "A Jury of
Her Peers."

Here is a piece of a legend I heard while living at Fort
Leavenworth, Kansas, while my husband attended the
Command and General Staff College. A stone house on the

post has been occupied by military families ever since it was built in the mid-eighteen hundreds. It is haunted. Apparently, a woman died alone in this house while her husband was away.

Count off in threes. For eight to ten minutes: all the ones write about the woman. Who was she? Why was she in Kansas? What did she die of? *All the twos: write about the husband.* Who was he, what was he doing in Kansas, and where was he while she was dying? *All the threes: write about how and why the house is haunted.* (For a sample writing, see Appendix, page 75.)

Read aloud what you have written, in sequences of three.

Twelve

REVISE A FAIRY TALE

Revise: to change or modify

MANY OF US GREW UP hearing and reading fairy tales, and internalizing the fantasy that the prince will come and save us and we will live happily ever after. Where did these fairy tales come from? The main themes seem to be a mixture of Celtic and Indian origin, which would help explain why more than 345 versions of "Cinderella" can be found between India and Ireland.

Some years ago, while studying Celtic mythology for a class, I came across a picture of a silver "bracelet" of Celtic origin, purportedly used for some socio-religious purpose, rather than for ornamentation. It formed a circle ending in two cow heads facing one another. It is nearly identical to a silver "bangle" sent to my daughter by her Indian grandmother: a circle ending in two elephant heads facing one another.

Whatever the origin of the fairy tales, they all contain elements of enchantment, magic, wonder. I share with you my silver bangle/bracelet. On difficult days it feels like a handcuff chaining me to the patriarchal expectations of my father's Ireland and my husband's India. On more positive days, it's a symbol of the strong goddess tradition that predates the patriarchy in each of these cultures.

Today, many women poets are revising the old fairy tales to reflect what really happens after the princess goes off to live in the prince's kingdom. Marge Piercy's "Story Wet As Tears" about the frog prince is ironically funny; Maxine Kumin's "The Archaeology of A Marriage" about Sleeping

Beauty fifty years later is sarcastically wistful; while Anne Sexton's book *Transformations* is outright chilling.

For eight to ten minutes, go back to your favorite childhood fairy tale and revise it to reflect your life now. If you need some "magic" to help you move forward, I loan you my silver bracelet/bangle. (For a sample writing, see Appendix, page 76.)

Read aloud what you have written.

Thirteen

REFORM A BIBLICAL STORY

Reform: to improve, as by alteration; to form again

OTHER STORIES THAT HAVE SHAPED US within our culture are to be found in *The Bible*. Whether we've been raised in the Judeo-Christian tradition or not, the metaphors, symbols, and images of *The Bible* live in our collective unconscious, and from there shape our lives without our always being aware of it. This is why my daughter found *The Bible* included on her college reading list for incoming freshman. And it is why, when my Hindu-raised husband was told by colleagues that he has "the patience of Job," he had to ask them to explain what they were talking about.

But what images do we, as women, internalize from *The Bible*? It is so clearly a book that is of, for, and by men. When we're included in it at all, it is in relationship to the male protagonists, as wives, mothers, sisters, daughters, whores. Our roles have been defined by the patriarchs and their male god.

Unlike the strong goddesses in the Hindu tradition of my husband or the Greek heritage I studied in sixth grade, few female figures in *The Bible* have any personalities or power of their own: all their energies are absorbed and utilized by the males, whether divine or human. We have, for instance, the mother of god, but not god the mother. The message that reverberates in our psyches is that feminine wisdom is of no account. We must play out our roles unquestioningly, in the image of meek and mild Mary, so that the begatting can continue. Mary pondered all things on the first Christmas Eve, and kept them in her heart. What if someone had thought to ask her what she was thinking or feeling?

For eight to ten minutes, re-write a story from The Bible *in which a woman appears, and this time retell it from her point of view. (For a sample writing, see Appendix, page 77.)*

Read aloud what you have written.

Fourteen

REVERSE WOMAN'S SIN

Reverse: to turn in the opposite direction, or order;
to exchange positions of; transpose

SUPPOSE WE READ *THE BIBLE* as metaphoric of men's life journeys? For instance, what if the life, death, and resurrection of Jesus can be interpreted as a map to be followed, by men, towards wholeness? If the psychologists are right that a boy's task is to separate from his mother by developing strong ego boundaries, in order to be about his "father's business," then at mid-life the male's task is to "crucify" the ego that keeps him separated from his larger Self. Therefore, the sel*fish*ness we read about in *The Bible* is the "sin" that keeps MAN from becoming whole.

But what about women's life journeys? While separating from mother, the girl still retains a sense of identification with the source of her being; she is never totally cut off from the sacred within. But she is continually pitched away from this center, her place of wholeness, when she lives the way society says she should: through relationships with others, selflessly. Her mid-life task then becomes the opposite of the man's. She needs to develop ego boundaries that will help her re-direct her energies inward, so that she may re-awaken the Self of wholeness. Self*less*ness is WOMAN's "sin."

This lack of a sense of self shows in many ways, as Valerie Saiving notes in her essay "The Human Situation" (in *Womanspirit Rising*): diffuseness, distractibility, dependence—yet instead of being encouraged to become a fully developed human being, a woman must deny her impulse towards wholeness if she would live out her role as defined by patriarchal religion and society.

For eight to ten minutes, write about SIN from a woman's perspective and experience. What cuts you off from your center and makes you feel scattered and unbalanced? For what do you need to be forgiven? What is your personal sin? (For a sample writing, see Appendix, top of page 78.)

Read aloud what you have written.

Fifteen

REALIZE THE UNIVERSAL

Realize: to comprehend completely; to make real

HOW DOES A WOMAN AWAKEN to the powers of being that connect her with the universe from within? In *Diving Deep and Surfacing*, Carol Christ suggests that the very sin of self negation prepares a woman for the mystical experience of enlightenment/awakening. Her weak ego boundaries leave her more open to the mystic experience of union and integration with the powers of being. Christ goes on to note that mystical identification occurs for women in nature; a solitary walk in the woods can bring insights that assure her she is on her right "path," and reaffirm her selfhood. Mystical AHA!s can also occur in community, especially in groups where women are empowering one another to name and value their experiences. And writing in a group, then sharing what's been written, reinforces this process.

Writing itself is a way to evoke mystical experience. Paying attention to the words you have put down on paper is akin to the mystic's concept of prayer as attention to God. It is no accident that mystics use metaphoric language to speak of that which can't be analyzed, only experienced. An inspired image, May Sarton tells us, is one that comes from below the surface of consciousness and points to what we really mean and know, not what we thought we knew.

For eight to ten minutes, imagine a natural object, something as specific as a grain of sand, a mustard seed, a tree (rather than the whole forest). Let that "part" become a symbol for the whole that opens up the world and, as Eliade puts it, helps us attain the universal. If you can hear the truth it has to tell you through the words you use to name it, you may experience a oneness with your natural object, and know its truth to be your own. Put your image into words. (For a sample writing, see Appendix, bottom of page 78.)

Read aloud what you have written.

Sixteen

RECLAIM THE MOON

Reclaim: to make suitable for cultivation or habitation

THERE'S SOME DEBATE as to whether or not women are closer to nature because of their biological cycles than men, who are always identified with "culture." But that's no wonder: the culture we live in was created of, for, and by men. This is why many women find that they must go off to the woods or out in the garden for a place where, among insects, birds, and the animals, they can be fully human. Is it possible that men created culture, beginning with initiation rites that emulated the natural blood-letting of women, as a way to deliberately exclude the women they were so jealous of?

Our patriarchal cultures continue to define and describe male life experience, and codify it in mythologies and religions. As Campbell reminds us, myths guide us, psychologically, through the stages of our lives. Psychology has finally verified what Hinduism has always known: adults go through distinct phases of life that require differing tasks, tests, and responsibilities. Hinduism divides these stages into child, student, householder, and grandfather—when the man goes off into the forest for spiritual renewal. The woman goes with him, but it is his life and his journey. Even the custom of suttee, in which the widow burns herself alive on her husband's funeral pyre, was required so that she would ensure their passage into eternity together.

But where do we turn to find images and symbols and metaphors and the myths reflecting women's life stages? Women have often been associated with the image of the moon: as the moon reflects the sun's light, so do women reflect back what isn't of their own power and making. The word "menstruation" itself comes from the monthly cycle of the moon.

For eight to ten minutes, write about the moon. What does that image say of, for, or to you? How do you react to the sight of a full moon? Where were you and what were you doing in July, 1969, when a man landed on the moon? (For sample writings, see Appendix, page 79.)

Read aloud what you have written.

Seventeen

REMEMBER MOTHERING

Remember: to recall to the mind, think of again; to retain in the mind; to keep (someone) in mind

THE WAXING, full, and waning phases of the moon have been represented in the image of the triple goddess: virgin, mother, crone. Remember the fairy tale in which the queen longs for a daughter with skin white as snow, cheeks red as blood, and hair black as ebony? These are the goddess's colors: virgin—pure white, mother—blood red, and crone—wisdom black.

You have already written about your childhood, that time when you were a maiden, like Persephone out in the meadow picking wildflowers (and Heidi?), before the ground opened up under her. You may want to go back and re-read what you wrote: it contains clues to the person you'll be called to become in the crone phase of your life.

But meanwhile, the mothering full-bellied full moon phase demands that we set aside our needs and desires and our own self-identity in order to anticipate and meet the needs of the child that is totally dependent on us for survival. The home is our second womb that nurtures our children until they can be on their own. The responsibility is awesome, and unrewarded, except by lip service, in patriarchal societies. And so we shall celebrate it ourselves, for the ability (and willingness) to transcend our own thoughts and needs and interests in order to meet the needs of the child is an invaluable skill, as well as a profound experience. How many times did we wake up in the middle of the night before the child started crying? We know what we know, and do what we do, and it is good.

For eight to ten minutes, name and value an experience you've had nurturing others. Joseph Campbell remembers an old Chinese saying: Mothers are the only gods in whom all the world believes. (For a sample writing, see Appendix, page 80.)

Read aloud what you have written.

REJECT DISTRACTIONS

> *Reject: to refuse to accept or grant; to discard,*
> *throw away*

OF COURSE there is a great danger of losing one's self
completely during this nurturing phase; this is the place
where selflessness becomes women's sin. I recall that, on the
psychiatric ward where once I worked, the overwhelming
majority of the patients were middle age, middle class
women, suffering from the "empty nest" syndrome. Drug
and electric shock therapies did not seem to help long-term;
these women were back on the unit, hospitalized with
depression, again and again. Without someone else to live
for and through, their lives lost all meaning. Yet, it is in this
phase of life that a woman, finally finished with enabling
others to live their lives, can fully become who she's meant
to be. But how? And do we dare? After all, our western
patriarchal culture burned over eight million women at the
stake over a three-hundred-year period of time because they
claimed their power and used their wisdom.

Perhaps the image of the waning moon can be interpreted
as the process of detaching and withdrawing into ourselves,
so that our energy may go into giving birth to ourSelves.

There is an old Chinese parable which says that a man's
task at mid-life is to go up the mountain and sit cross-
legged, his hands on his thighs in the *up* position: saying yes
to all the parts of himself he ignored, denied, or didn't
develop while he was focussing on his career. But, the
parable continues, a woman's task at mid-life is to go up the
maintain and sit cross-legged, her hands on her thighs in the
down position, putting her energy back into her own body,

and saying the great, creative NO to all that has kept her pitched away from her center.

For eight to ten minutes, write down what you will say the great NO to. Or perhaps you need to say YES to some things in order to become more fully yourself. (For a sample writing, see the Appendix, page 81.)

Read aloud what you have written.

Nineteen

REPOSE IN THE DARKNESS

Repose: to lie at rest, relax; to place, as faith and trust in

THERE IS, of course, another phase of the moon: the fourth
stage, that of total darkness. It can be seen metaphorically as
"the dark night of the soul," that "never-never land" where
the old life has been lost or given up or out-grown and the
new one hasn't fully emerged yet. The moon three days dark
is analogous to Christ's three days in the tomb. In many
cultures, the moon is the place where souls go after death, to
be judged and either sent on to heaven, or back to earth in a
new incarnation. This brings to mind the concept of purga-
tory where one is cleansed of one's sins in order to be born
into a new life. In any case, the moon can be viewed as a
place of transformation; its darkness symbolizes fertility,
inspiration, and immortality. As M. Ester Harding tells us in
Women's Mysteries, the moon is the lesser light which rules
the night of instinct and the inner, intuitive world within
each of us.

As a writer, I find there's a "dark night of the soul" within
the creative process. It is known as "writer's block," and is a
period of supreme frustration when a project one has been
intensely involved with refuses to move forward. No matter
how hard one tries, one cannot get from point A, the stage
of preparation, to point E, the vaguely sensed end product.
There is only one course of action, and that is to abandon
the project: give up, give in, let it go, i.e., put it completely
out of one's mind, while one does something completely
different. The problem then sinks down into another level of
consciousness, and remains there, brooding, simmering,

working itself out, incubating, hibernating in that fertile, moon-dark, instinctive space.

Realizing that for many, life is not a strictly linear journey, but a series of cycles (like the moon?) that spiral backwards to re-work unresolved issues before moving forward, *what experience(s) of "the dark night of the soul" have you had?* Or, how do you imagine it to be? *Write for eight to ten minutes.* (For a sample writing, see the Appendix, page 82.)

Read aloud what you have written.

Twenty

RESPOND TO ANIMATION

Respond: to react positively

WHO OR WHAT WILL SAVE YOU from "the dark night of the soul," rescue you from the abyss, carry you into the new life? In ancient cultures, the savior figures were female: Isis, Ishtar, Inanna. And there are surviving Irish folk tales in which the female voluntarily descends into hell to rescue the male. This makes sense on a psychological level. The soul has always been recognized as feminine, even in patriarchal religions; for the male to be psychologically "whole" he must be in relationship with the feminine within his own psyche. Jung named this the anima: she is man's INspiration, the muse guiding his creation.

But what of the woman experiencing "the dark night of the soul?" Because she IS female, she is one with the mysterious source of her being, but she doesn't always know, feel, or believe it. The male part of her psyche, the animus, is not her inspiration. As Irene Claremont de Castillejo explains in *Knowing Woman*, the animus' task is merely to show the woman what is already there, within herself. When she has been pitched away from her center and lost in the abyss, he is the spirit that fans the dying embers back to life in her being. He is not the goal of the journey she must make to be whole; rather, he is a Hermes figure standing at the cross-roads, showing her the direction in which she must go, alone. If she stops to make a relationship with him, she will not get to where she's meant to go.

We women usually become aware of the animus figure within our psyches when we project it onto a real man in our lives. We suddenly find ourselves irrationally attracted to someone we are not, can not, should not be married to. He becomes what John Sanford calls "the invisible partner" in our lives; we obsess, fantasize, and dream about him almost against our will.

For eight to ten minutes, describe the man you fantasize about; the one who so stirs you up that he awakens parts of you which you thought/felt were long dead; the one who animates your being; your animus. (For sample writings, see the Appendix, page 83.)

Read aloud what you have written.

Twenty-one
RECREATE YOURSELF

Recreate: to create anew

THERE IS A TERRIBLE DANGER of being "carried away" by the projected animus figure, and again distracted from our goal: reaching that place deep within where we are again whole. Any "marriage" with the animus figure must take place within the psyche, not out in the real world. Only then can the journey towards transformation continue. The "marriage" within the psyche produces the Divine Child: the spiritual self. For the woman the goal is to become "virgin" again, just as the new moon is reborn from the darkness. The word "virgin" here refers to its original meaning: spiritual (not biological) intactness. To become virgin again means a woman becomes "one-in-herself."

This parallels the creative process I began discussing earlier. The attraction to, union with, and fertilization by the animus figure within the woman's psyche leads to that time of incubation within that moon-dark place below the level of consciousness. In its own time (just like a real baby!) the solution to the creative problem reveals itself, most often when you least expect it, such as in the middle of the night. This illumination (the moon's light?), with continued hard work, can bring forth something altogether new: a poem, a book, an invention, a scientific theory, a social action.

Metaphorically, the process feels like Persephone's return from the underworld to be reunited with her Mother, so the earth will burst forth from winter into spring. It's the sheer magic, wonder and surprise of that first spring flower you see . . .

43

For eight to ten minutes, name and develop your metaphor for rebirth, reincarnation, renewal, resurrection. (For sample writings, see Appendix, page 84.)

Read aloud what you have written.

Twenty-two
REVEAL HEAVEN HERE AND NOW

Reveal: to make known

WE EXPERIENCE GLIMPSES of the "new" self that is
possible during moments of at-one-ment, inner peace,
profound joy, or even the wonder of going outside again
after being stuck in the house with the flu, ill ourselves and/
or nursing sick family members. Everything looks suddenly
different: fresh and new. We see things we hadn't noticed or
appreciated before. They were there all the time, but something had to happen within us before we could truly see.
This brings to mind the *Gnostic Gospel According to Thomas*
in which Jesus promises us that the kingdom of heaven is
spread upon the earth if we would but see it. In other words,
the eternal, the no where, is really now here: it just depends
on your perspective, or where you place the "w."

In his final book, *The Inner Reaches of Outer Space:
Metaphor As Myth And As Religion*, Joseph Campbell assures
us we can live in both the eternal and temporal worlds
simultaneously through metaphor; the symbols of the sacred
interpreted poetically and psychologically, rather than
literally, give us a sense of actual participation in the Infinite,
the Transcendent. In short, a metaphor, because it implies a
relationship between two differing things, changes our
comprehension of them both. It begins with something
concrete and carries it outward, to new and unpredictable
places. The surprise at the other end comes as an Aha!, a
revelation that transcends the individual personality.

For eight to ten minutes, try to find a metaphor that names how you feel when you experience your "new" self. In other words, what is your image of heaven, paradise, the Garden of Eden? How does the world look and feel when you are centered, at one with yourself? (For a sample writing, see the Appendix, page 85.)

Read aloud what you have written.

Twenty-three
RESIST HELL'S TRAPPINGS

Resist: to strive or work against; to withstand

OF COURSE YOU KNOW what's coming next: there's no way we can speak metaphorically of "heaven" without also naming our personal metaphors for "hell."

Hell is often depicted in comics as a place red with flames. For me, flaming red symbolizes anger, my personal experience of hell. I get trapped in anger when I feel invisible, unvalued, and taken for granted or advantage of. I become angry when I feel my "new" self being sucked back into old, untransformed behavior that keeps me in the role of victim, i.e., being acted upon, rather than taking positive action. And I fly into an absolute rage whenever I come across yet another example of how my society subtly undermines women's positive self image.

For example, the recent March for Women's Lives here in Washington drew well over the estimated half a million people. At least ninety percent of us were females. Yet, when the local paper reported the event, it led off with a quote from a white middle class, middle aged male saying the march was a good thing and that the political leaders of the country ought to take notice. This particular male is a church member friend whom I admire, and agree with. But from my perspective as a feminist, I interpret the media's quoting him as needing a (white) male to legitimize women's rights, issues, and concerns. And this infuriates me. But if I express my anger, I'll be perceived as a castrating bitch/witch who ought to be grateful that men marched in support of women at all, and that the paper even bothered to report the event. Instead, I'm resentful. I identify with Kali,

Hindu goddess of destruction, often depicted as a hideous hag, dancing on her husband's corpse, devouring his entrails.

For eight to ten minutes, explore your personal metaphor for hell. You don't have to act it out; write it instead. (For sample writings, see the Appendix, page 86.)

Read aloud what you have written.

Twenty-four

RETURN TO DO WHAT

Return: to come back; to respond

NOW WHAT? Do you stay stuck in your "hell," or do you
learn what it's trying to teach you, and move on? Kali's
destructiveness is for a purpose: to break down the old and
make way for the new. But often, as women, we internalize
our "hell," blame ourselves for our pain, and thereby
reinforce our powerlessness to live the lives we are meant to
live.

This is even reflected in our literature. In *Archetypal
Patterns in Women's Fiction*, Annis Pratt notes that spiritual
journeys which give birth to strong, powerful, autonomous,
transformed women often end in punishment, rather than
reward. Women are more than likely driven mad or to
suicide when they try to reintegrate themselves into society.
Society simply isn't ready to receive the woman who returns
from the mountaintop with her dream.

So, do we give up and give in—or change society so that
we can live out full, meaningful lives? Why shouldn't society
reflect our values and meet our needs: we make up more
than half of it! Yet everything in it—from the personal
(family structures) to the political (the structures of govern-
ment, religion, the economy, even the legal system)—is
constructed around the needs and values of men, AS IF
THEIR PERSPECTIVES WERE THE WHOLE PICTURE.
I remember when I was working on my peace studies
degree. I was an army wife at the time, and the commander
took me aside at a party and told me how much he admired
what I was doing but went on to assure me that "war is

simply a part of human nature." I didn't know then, but do know now, that I should have replied, "Speak for yourself!"

For eight to ten minutes, name something you would change in your world so you would feel at home in it. Let your imagination go. And why not? If we don't have a vision to work towards, we will never begin the process of moving forward. We will stay stuck in "hell." (For sample writings, see the Appendix, page 87.)

Read aloud what you have written.

Twenty-five
REQUIRE CHANGES

Require: to need; to demand, insist upon

ONE WAY TO BEGIN MAKING CHANGES in the outside world is to accept, honor, and value what we need as women. Until and unless we take ourselves seriously, "they" won't, either. Becoming "one of the boys" and playing by their rules changes nothing; it just makes us complicit in maintaining the status quo. Instead, we must listen to our own inner voices when we find ourselves uncomfortable in male-constructed situations. What does it mean if we find ourselves anxious, upset, or depressed in roles that seem so natural for men? Perhaps they're not so "natural" for women.

For example, I am acutely aware of being almost physically ill whenever I walk into a university classroom to teach. I don't have all the answers to anything, only a little more knowledge and experience than (most of) my students. Yet they look up to me as a voice of authority. And I always feel like a fraud; I describe my teaching style as "bluffing." My male colleagues assure me that everyone feels that way. Everyone is, in fact, bluffing, all the way to the top of the hierarchy. (Now there's a scary thought!) Mercifully, I've recently come across Peggy McIntosh's article, "Feeling Like Fraud," in which she assures me that my discomfort comes from being put in a hierarchical role. As a woman, I long ago internalized that I don't deserve to be in a position of authority: the majority of people I've observed at the top of anything have been men. Women don't belong there. Plus, women don't LIKE being there. It's not so much that women CAN'T stand behind podiums, McIntosh tells us, as that we women can't STAND podiums! YES!, for me, YES!!

So now what? Do I stay out of the classroom because I'm uncomfortable? Or do I evolve a style of teaching that is non-hierarchical, one that is more of a partnership style of learning?

For eight to ten minutes, identify something required of you in our patriarchal society that makes you uncomfortable. Examine it. Accept your discomfort as a clue to what could and should be changed. (For sample writings, see the Appendix, page 88.)

Read aloud what you have written.

RECALL A HISTORICAL WOMAN

Recall: to call back, ask or order to return; to remember

WHERE DO WE LOOK for stories of self-actualized women leading authentic, valued lives in which we can see our own struggles reflected? Certainly, you may have noticed, not in our history books. Many years ago, a writing mentor recommended that I read Hendrik Van Loon's *The Story of Mankind* and study his use of language: the book had won the first Newbery Medal awarded for excellence in children's books. I was depressed for days after reading it. It was a narrative of continuous warfare. What a tragic commentary on human history! Now, many years later, I finally realize it was only a partial history: the story of MANkind, white, Western mankind.

What were the women doing throughout the thousands of years of (male) recorded history? Elise Boulding sets out to explore this in her seven hundred-plus page volume, *The Underside of History*, A View of Women Through Time. For without a past, we have no present, much less a future: we do not see ourselves as participants in the human experience! One of the biggest aha!'s for me in Elise's book was reading that the suffrage movement came about because women, who were trying to deal with the negative social impact of increasing industrialization, suddenly realized they needed access to political power in order to affect change. For centuries women have carried the moral values of society, but in order to fully carry them out, women need to be out in the public sphere, rather than stuck on a pedestal and sentimentalized for our "superior" natures, while treated as inferior members of society. The suffragettes not only won the vote for us, they got us into the history books, if only a line that mentions that in 1920, men "gave" us the vote. An alternate book I use with Peace Studies students, *The Power of the People, Active Nonviolence in the United States* (300 years of "hidden" history!), includes a picture of a suffragette being force fed at Lorton Prison.

Can we bring women from history forward into our own lives to serve as mentors and friends? Is there a woman in history with whom you have an affinity? *For eight to ten minutes, make some connections between your lives, honoring you both.* (For sample writings, see the Appendix, page 89.)

Read aloud what you have written.

Twenty-seven

RECONCILE YOUR WORLD-VIEW

Reconcile: to make compatible or consistent

AFTER NEARLY FIFTY YEARS of struggling for women's right to vote, Elizabeth Cady Stanton called together a committee of thirty women scholars to re-evaluate the passages of *The Bible* that either referred to women or excluded women. She had come to realize that the sexist language, symbols, and stories in *The Bible* were being used to reinforce and legitimize men's determination to keep women in an inferior position in society. Stanton and her scholars dared to believe that sexism existed in *The Bible* because it had been interpreted by men: fallible men. For example, when they went back to the original Hebrew word for creator they found it was not "Yahweh," but "Elohim," a plural word that can refer to either male or female god or gods. The result of their work, published in 1895, is known as *The Woman's Bible*.

Women in religion today, nearly a hundred years later, have made great progress in having inclusive language used in church liturgy, hymns, and Biblical readings. But merely including the feminine pronoun in front of male terms such as power, glory, dominion, judge, ruler, kingdom, omnipotent, everlasting, almighty, etc., leaves me as alienated as ever. Would the *Old Testament* read like such a war epic, with the Hebrews forever putting everything "to the sword" as commanded by Yahweh, if, in the beginning, the creator had truly been equally female?

The great mother goddess of pre-patriarchal times created everything out of her own body, rather than standing outside of creation, one step removed, saying "Let there be . . ." She was in the world, and of it, as it was of her.

For eight to ten minutes, write a creation story out of the feminine matrix, your world-view perspective as a woman. (For sample writings, see the Appendix, page 90.)

Read aloud what you have written.

Twenty-eight

RESTORE YOUR IMAGE OF THE SACRED

Restore: to bring back into existence or use

IN *THE UNDERSIDE OF HISTORY*, Boulding writes that because every society develops its own symbols to support its view of the cosmos and the place of people within it, patriarchal cultures build subordinate images of women into the cosmologies and creation stories, and then rationalize their treatment of women accordingly. Men's dualistic viewpoint of women as "other" keeps us out of the mainstream of God-the-Father sanctioned political (i.e., public sphere) power; we are out in the margins along with all the "others": children, slaves, men of color, etc. And, meanwhile, the cosmology that gives MAN dominion over all the earth now threatens to destroy the planet economically, environmentally, militarily, and spiritually. We desperately need the balance of the feminine perspective if we are to survive as a species.

The divine feminine wisdom that was swallowed by the patriarchy 5,000 years ago is re-emerging today, calling us to affirm what we as women intuitively know: that all life is interconnected and sacred. But this only happens as we women speak up for our values and visions, in both the private and the public spheres. Only as we begin to questions men's definitions of right and wrong, as Carol Gilligan does in *In A Different Voice*, will we be able to re-name, re-define, re-create, re-vise (see again) the world as it can be.

Women studying religion have come to realize that a theologian's gender has a lot to do with her/his theological conclusions. And they have come to the conclusion that the first principle of theology "done" from a woman's perspective is the personal experience of the sacred. Unlike male theologians who name god as separate from themselves, just as they separated from mother in childhood, women theologians often retain a sense of oneness with the source of their being. Therefore, their experience of the divine/ultimate/sacred differs from male experience.

For eight to ten minutes, write about a word, image, symbol, or metaphor that names the sacred for you. (For sample writings, see the Appendix, page 91.)

Read aloud what you have written.

Twenty-nine
RESOLVE TO CONTINUE

Resolve: to make a decision about, firmly

MANY WOMEN EXPERIENCE the sacred deep within themselves, at the very core of their being. It is there that the feminine wisdom survives: ancient, hidden, powerful. You have begun to tap into that place with your writing. It happens whenever what comes out onto the page is not what you started to write. It happens whenever the words on the page set you off in a totally different direction from where you thought you were headed. It happens whenever the process of writing itself connects your inner and outer world so that you experience a profound sense of wholeness, joy, and inner peace.

Will you continue to give voice to the feminine spirit within you? Are you willing to set aside eight to ten minutes a day a few times a week to sit, in silence, in a sacred space and, with your pen, open the channel to that place of grace? As May Sarton assures us in *Writings on Writing*, we can cultivate inspiration, awareness, and the state of being fully awake. But it takes discipline. Just as a mystic induces awareness through prayer, fasting, silence, etc., a writer must develop her own disciplines that open her to being in tune with (intuiting) that which is both within and beyond her self. What do you need to do in order to feed your spirit and nourish the process? Whatever it is, you must make a conscious commitment to yourself to do it, or else you will go do the laundry, wash the dishes, clean out the refrigerator instead. And that is precisely the problem: we women have spent so much of our lives doing the endless, mundane, time-consuming tasks that divert us from what we need to do for ourSelves that our stories go untold, our values unnamed, our spirits unnourished. And so, the world we live in continues to reflect only men's lives and perspectives.

Writing is an act of the ego. It asserts your right to exist, as well as your existence itself. Walt Whitman created himself in his poem "Song of Myself." And the Celtic poet Amairgen, upon coming to the shores of Ireland, chanted, "I am the wind that blows o'er the sea; / I am the save of the deep." *For eight to ten minutes, begin with the words "I am" and go on.* (For sample writings, see the Appendix, page 92.)

Read aloud what you have written.

Thirty
RESHAPE YOUR OWN NAMING

Reshape: to give new form to; to develop

NOW, how to keep going? Before you are tempted to say that you have nothing else to write about, let me say "nonsense!" You've barely begun. If you look back over all that you've written in response to the suggested exercises, you'll find you've got a body of work to continue with. Eight to ten minutes is barely enough time to get something started. You can go back to each of your writings and revise it, see it again. But one word of advice: please don't discard any of the versions you do of a work, especially the original. Your final revision may say something very different from what you first draft wanted to say; you may need or want to go back to the original impulse.

There are several techniques you can use to open up what's already been written, to reveal new insights or deepen what's already there. You can expand a piece by playing with strong words within it and letting them open up into images and symbols larger than you thought you intended. You can condense a piece by taking out weak words (like adjectives) and thereby making the whole tighter and stronger. You can rearrange lines to let them play off one another in new ways. You can go back to a strong phrase that people responded to (with gasps, ahas, or giggles) and begin a new piece with that as a first line. You can repeat lines like a chant or an echo, and polish your lines so they have a rhythmic sound. You can substitute words that play off one another alliteratively.

You can continue reading your work aloud, for affirmation, feedback, and a sense of rightness of its sound to yourself, as well as to others. The women at my church have used their writing as the basis for women's worship services. Not only did they hear their own experiences and insights valued, but they evoked other women's celebration of their own insights and experiences.

As a final exercise here, and the beginning of your continuing effort, retrieve a piece you have already written and begin to revise it. Use line breaks and stanza spacing to set off key images and insights so you experience them in a new, perhaps more intense, way. (For a sample writing, see the Appendix, page 93.)

Read aloud what you have written.

CONCLUSION

THE IDEA FOR DEVELOPING THIS WORKSHOP began back in 1985, when I attended a women and religion retreat. Nearly every woman there admitted she had written at some time or other in her life, but had never shared what she'd written with anyone. If you have done these exercises in a group, you've already gone beyond that. If you have done these exercises alone, you are continuing the tradition of diary, journal, and letter writing that has been the source of our knowledge about women's lives throughout recorded history. Will you continue?

You can decide to destroy what you've written and will write as you revise from this work. You can hide your work safely away in your room, as did Emily Dickinson. Dissuaded from publishing more than a handfull of poems in her lifetime, Dickinson sewed the rest of her poems together into little packets, and kept them in boxes in her room. After her death, her sister-in-law and her publisher found them—1,775 poems in all. Together, they edited her "quaint" punctuation and capitalization, and published their version of her work. It was nearly one hundred years later that her poems were published the way she had written them—finally. Meanwhile, her contemporary and literary equal, Walt Whitman, was publishing and promoting his own work.

Will you choose to promote your vision and values through your word and your actions? I welcome your insights and input on how that might become a reality.

IN OTHER WORDS

• ONE

Joan Starr in transition again.
Mother with a vengeance.
Passionate teacher.
Emotional, intuitive, mystic.
Rather typical for my time and place.
Brooklyn born and energized in big city international culture.
Word lover, reverence for written words, and pages.
Stories are cherished companions and memories are stored
from questing journeys.

Name: Ada from my grandmother and Katherine from my other grandmother, something I hated as a girl but now regard as a nice way to be tied in with my beginnings.

Height: too much, once, I felt awkward, gangly, somehow or other my arms and legs never went in manageable directions. Now, it's nice to be tall, able to see above some parts of the crowd, able to wear "tall people" clothes.

Age: getting older, for which I am grateful, and with added years is coming a sense of mellowness that is new and easier to live with than the obligations of my youth.

Eye: grey to blue to green depending on what I wear, the weather, my mood—real barometers of the situation I am in.

Ada Churchill

• TWO

I am the oak that never sheds its leaves
for I've known no dormant seasons.
My roots have found their way deep into
the earth. They anchor me as their
invisible tentacles suck nutrients for my soul.

My branches stretch to the warm sunshine.
At times they grow to a space where I am
not wanted. They cut me back. I become
crooked, unbalanced. And then, from the wound,
I grow new buds, to twigs, to branches
reaching once again for the sunshine.

I have good growing seasons.
But have also suffered blight.
Many times and for many years
I've been the host to other living
creatures. Some grateful for my nurturing.
Some wanting only to suck my juices dry
and leave me hollow. And yet I stand just the same—
but forever changing.

                              Miriam Phoebe Newton

Image

I have flown as a butterfly
Soared as a hawk
Played at being a mirror
Reflecting surfaces,
Coiled snake-like forming a circle
Mouth to tail.

Now, I am a web-spinner
Trying to leave patterns
To mark the places I have been.
To leave a trace, a mark that I was here
To share with those to come a hint
Of what the journey has been like
I'm seeking a thread with tensile strength
To keep my fragile lacelike work
From disappearing before it's read.

                              Joan Starr

THREE

In the Beginning

and I am washing, ironing, rehanging perma-press
curtains, before spring classes begin

always before I've done this to silence
the voice of my mother in the back of my mind

I know now
there's no voice,
just the act:

Barbara scouring bathrooms
two days before surgery

Peggy scrubbing the floor
on the day she left her husband

Mother eight months pregnant with a seventh child
cleaning the corners of upstairs windows with a toothbrush

why this propitiation?

ask Marsha why she made the beds
before driving the wrong way down the highway.

GCR

• FOUR

Perhaps the tree I knew most intimately was the one that bore apples every summer during my third to tenth years. My sister Cathy and I would climb that tree, sprawl out on its smooth curved limbs, wrap our silky legs around its hard core. We would pick the apples, eat a few, but most were transformed into Mother's succulent apple pies. The apple tree was home, a play place, a nest for squirrel-like girls in their early years.

Years later it was another tree that helped me choose Cathy's grave—a graceful, towery eucalyptus, its leaves like tiny flags waving against a deep blue California sky. Beneath that tree we laid my sister's body to rest—and it is thus that I know trees to be sentinels of life, and death. In the case of the eucalyptus, that tree helps me know Cathy lives on forever—in the tree's roots and branches, in the wind that dances through its leaves, and in my heart.

Carolyn Cottom

Tree

If there is an afterlife, may I become a tree—magnificent, reliable, asymmetrical, growing, changing, essentially there—always predictable, and welcoming, enveloping, and free.

If I could paint it would be trees. Sentinels of the earth, my own Lord of the Heavens. Elegant asymmetry unfolding endlessly without restraint, without warning, impulsively, playfully, and mysteriously—one branch into another into another until adorned by leaves or seasonal bouquets.

Jeanne Gayler

• FIVE

A snake gently twists across
the sloping desert
    tracing
the passionate spirals
and undulations of women's
curves on the swelling sand.
    The silent wind creeps
behind
    erasing our serpentine
forms with dusty breaths.
A desert enigma of lost journeys,
and hidden hieroglyphs
as infinite as sand,
    as infinite as women's words.

                                     Katherine Bartov

SIX

On the Eve

of the equinox
first menses calls
a young daughter
out of childhood,
the moon sheds its shadow
the serpent its skin
and Eve is expelled
from the Garden
again.

Rites of passage
for this generation
take place on the track
a baton passed on in a race
her team sister gives
her a rose the same shade
of the stain on her sheets:
this "messiness"
connects her with
the Eastern-block athletes
at the Munich Olympics
beseiging the doctor
for whole boxes of pads

then the hostages taken
no way to save them
but to try cyanide
shot in by canister
if all dropped simultaneously
Herr Doktor could
rush in, revive
with his antidote, his life's
research proved
if not
the headlines would
read "German Doctor
Gasses Jews
Again" instead
in a splatter of blood
the Israeli's pass
back into the Garden

Now this daughter
dreams the Olympics
and, with the startle
of blood, of becoming
a mother.

GCR

• SEVEN

Images of raucous wonderful birthday parties from pictures and
eight mm movies made by my Uncle Bill show a child with a blazing
aura, and tons of energy. I taught neighborhood kids how to ride bikes;
I raced, swung from ropes over the water, flew across the frozen bay in
winter—on skates, holding a sheet—rode on ice boats, crewed on
sailboats, climbed up on the roof of my parents' house, down trees—
all wildness, and then it all began to change for me by about the eighth
grade.

Cassie Arnold

Rebel!

Damned if I'd sit in Mama's parlor and eat those goddamned
little, white-bread sandwiches with the crusts all cut off,
or make rainbow colored jello-moulds to pass around to the
ladies, who plucked their eyebrows to look like Tallulah Bankhead!

Off I'd go to climb my tree with a bag of green plums and the
latest sex novel I'd snitched from under my aunt's bed. Safe—
set astride those limbs. High, high above the gushy, asinine
silliness—lovely, sinful delicious feeling of superiority.
Alone, away from the babble and the trivia.

I knew what would happen if I got caught and dragged out
to be paraded around, with all the ladies exclaiming: "Oh,
look at her big brown eyes"—the hives, that's what would
happen: fat, fiery, itchy welts, my own body physically
announcing its rebellion. Every corpuscle saying NO!

Jeanne Gayler

EIGHT

Because of the Starving

It begins when you're made to clean up your plate because
people are starving in _____ fill in the blank. For me, it was India.

From then on, you're haunted. Gaunt possibilities squat on
emaciated legs; dark eyes stare at those grains of rice

you are wasting. Their village stands in perpetual drought: land's
parcelled out so no irrigation schemes work. The women do double

work in the fields, in their families, yet find time to paint.
Their walls picture Rama's wife Sita carried off by the demon

Ravanna in a palanquin, or today's bride, after puberty, being
carried to her husband's village, painted by Sita Devi, who was

married off at age twelve to a poor Brahmin priest, four daughters
dying in childhood, too undernourished (as girls often are) to fight

off the cholera. In despair, their mother turns to the powerful
Durga, and recites her a poem-prayer daily, and paints, the way

she once painted on her arms, her school slate, on the ground;
then was punished for wasting time. Now, during Bihar's 1968

famine from drought she's discovered. When she exhibits in Delhi
will Durga protect her so no one will cut off her hands out of jealousy?

Her son comes with her to D.C., eats ice cream with every meal,
even breakfast—just like my husband when he first came from India.

But I'd rather talk of philosophy, religion, abstract ideas, yet
reality intrudes. When I'm in India, I cover my plate with my

hands, rudely refusing what I might waste—because of the starving.

GCR

• NINE

Family Stories

Family stories entertained us before television,
movies, radio, the Roxy or Broadway shows.
We were scribes in Egypt, hence the name Siegel,
(Sigilium, the sealer). We were writers.
Mother's father rode the Russian plains on a white horse.
Grandpa was the beloved, handsome, tall, improper, skeptic.
Grandma was the practical, yet romantic, reader of French
novels, a believer in love and adventure but condemned to
carry the weight of an orphaned family as a young widow with the door
to adventure closed. But she was the grandma who found health spas
and world fairs and far away markets and bargains and wholesale houses
when her children were grown and had her own business.
Dad's father was a dapper Romanian, lover of women, sirer of half
brothers and sisters from four or five alliances, who had one of the first
cars in Philadelphia and a thriving business and
my father, the entertainer, was the Marine hero who showed those
southern boys on Okinawa that a New York City kid named Siegel could
stand his ground and kill as well as any backwoods hunter.

Joan Starr

• TEN

On All Hallow's E'en

I cut up this
harvest-moon/pumpkin
and plunge my hands
into all orange, the color
of strength and endurance,
slimy and cold
as the corpse that
my daughter dissects
in anatomy lab.

Now I place
a small candle
inside, try to
light it. It
flickers, goes out.
I try again,
singe my fingers
and smell my own flesh.
Heretic!
        Witch?
Fire gleams
through these eyes I've
created, turns the grin
into a leer.

                    GCR

• ELEVEN

The woman

She was a merchant. She was a very open, loving person with three children. She'd managed to make her two stores thrive and was well known in town.

One afternoon while she was at home alone, a knock came at the back door. Before she even had time to respond, he was through the door. A vagrant-type burst into the room and bludgeoned her to death, then punctured her body with knife stabs.

Cassie Arnold

The husband

Her husband was a trader. When the cavalry went out on an expedition, he followed at a safe distance, trading his goodies with the Indians behind the cavalry lines.

One time he was trading when the cavalry suddenly retreated, with hostile Indians in pursuit, and he was stuck there. Now he was outside the protection of the U.S. Army, and to survive he lived with the Indians and eventually became one of them.

He even married an Indian woman. It was expected of him, of course! Besides, who could tell whether he'd ever get back to that old hag at the Army post! By the time he returned, she was dead.

Rhea Kahn

The haunting

He haunts himself, really, with his own twisted love of her, and his guilt. He opens the door between the worlds because, as the Navaho believe, a dark wind blows in his heart and she is only answering his call.

He can smell her sometimes and feel her in a room. When he concentrates she's gone. That's what is making him so crazy. He can't control it. It controls him. The dark wind holds them together.

Marsha Campbell

• TWELVE

In This Forest

Daily, I'm drawn
to this forest. Antlered
deer stare at me
through the trees, and I
think of Snow
White, the movie my real
mother took me to see.
I was sure we were going
instead to the dentist; after all,
it was Sunday, and movies
were sinful. Now in this
forest's silence of spider webs
dripping white mist, I recall
the awakening, feel
the apple dislodge from my throat,
sit up to look through
the glass dome. But I have
been silent so long, how
will I tell of this snake,
those frogs squawking into the water,
or these heron,
blue-grey in their hiding?

                    GCR

• THIRTEEN

Lot's Wife

Traveling never has gotten me anywhere.
Always uprooted like a common onion
shedding old identities
    the certain security of the solid kitchen table
    the garden plot I nurtured with my own hands and dreams
    the familiar spring water, succulent and cool
    the friends to sustain me through each calamity.
Since the beginning, you see,
I've played his shadow
    rooted to him
        faceless
            with no name
merely Lot's wife
as much a part of his life
as Lot's coat or Lot's shoes.
There have even been times
when I've been boxed into silence
by his hardhanded decree:
"It will be better for us in _____
    Fill in the blank—
    any city or country will do.
Prosperity, for him,
is always over the next hill
and like lemmings
we follow this strange call.
As time has edged along, though,
we've become more distant.
Each move has been a cutting away
        discarding unused dreams
        turning our backs on withered entanglements.
Often I've lingered behind him
wanting to remember the laughter of a neighbor's child
        the buzz of the fruit market
        the chant of the spice dealer
and all the while I've longed
to claim and preserve
the daily harvests of my own life
    with more than mere memories
    or the heart-hardening salt of these tears.

                Lenny Lianne

• FOURTEEN

My Sin

My sin has always been to devalue my own thoughts and feelings. As a child victim of incest, threatened with death if I told, I very quickly stockpiled my real thoughts and feelings. My mother, not consciously aware of what was happening, as far as I know, became my father's accomplice—an accomplice because she was not my ally.

How would I gain affirmation for my thinking and feeling if I'd only hold all inside, afraid for my own life?

Throughout my growing-up years I held thoughts and feelings close to me, protected them with my body, the pain locked in my cells. I could not outwardly be angry, although I could cry and not be abused for it. So when I became a teenager, I did a lot of crying—crying ostensibly for my mother and my parents' dissolving relationship—crying for me as a victim of their disintegrating marriage.

Not until I was forty did I uncover the memories of incest—when a string of memories came to me in a workshop designed for individual and personal healing.

Since then, I have begun to discover just how much I devalued myself—and have begun to hold my feelings and thoughts in greater and greater esteem. Nevertheless, this remains the great sin of my life: there are places where I still hold out, hold onto this sin in subtle ways.

Debbie Taylor

• FIFTEEN

A butterfly symbolizes the cosmos for me. The metamorphosis of this insect in many ways parallels the constant changing, evolving force of the universe. In the pupae stage, so much of what is happening is hidden, unknown, just like the movements of continental plates, earthquakes, volcanoes. In the caterpillar stage we see something most people want to squash, or birds eat them or they eat all the leaves off the trees. A very destructive or be destroyed stage—like storms, natural disasters, floods, heavy winds, avalanches. And then the butterfly emerges—a beautiful creature that gardeners try to attract into their yards with special plants. Frail creatures that soon soar to the heavens—like spirits. Ancient myths of many places thought butterflies were dead souls, waiting to be reborn. Butterflies are that spark in the cosmos that is the connecting tissue between souls.

Ada Churchill

• SIXTEEN

The Moon is the face in my dark. My dark, which is deep
inside me, seeming (like the night sky) to have no end,
no door. The night sky is the vast nothingness of my soul,
and I am lost in it.
   My grief seems to have no end when
   I am lost in it, and seems to carry
   me nowhere.
Then, suddenly, there is a face in the dark,
and the moon of my knowing begins to traverse
the dark like a chariot, not of fire, but of ice.
Frozen water, illumination of a still quiet moment—
frozen for me to see and grasp it, like a still and silent
snapshot. The insight may be brief but I am able to
capture it with my pen, thank God.
   Just as the moon, in a photo, holds a moment
of illumination *still* for me to *remember*:
   to remember who I am: a *soul with a face*,
   a face in my eternal dark.
   Now I turn my face to the sun—source of my light.
For it is true that without the sun I would wither and die.
Oh sun, light my moon face, help me to see in this dark
nothingness. Give my moon the true knowledge that
I am alive, even in the darkest night.

                                   Carolyn Cottom

The Moon

All would up around her, born under her sign, I get excited to see her
return. I call the others and we stand as she beams down that magic
connection.

Gradually, she slips away. Her fullness is enveloped by the creeping
darkness. Her bright face is shaded and she casts a dimmer light. The
moon cycles around and comes back.

I think of many moons, bright or brooding, cloud-surrounded, or
moving across a clear deep and uncloud-fettered background.

Sometimes that small sliver of its last remnant seems to cut through the
cosmos, creating just enough opening through which it does pour itself
to fullness, on schedule, and start it all anew.

                                   Cassie Arnold

• SEVENTEEN

Motherhood

I often tell my children they are the best thing that ever happened to me. And they are. Being a mother has been so healing to me. I find I'm mothering myself in mothering them. That doesn't seem to make sense when you think of how much energy and patience they require, but I remember how taking a walk with a toddler slowed me down. Made me notice important things. Made me breathe easier and fuller. Made me feel whole and at peace. Both my children have the habit of coming to sit on my lap, upon awakening. And I sit there with this heavy, scented, warm bundle and can feel my heart beat as my child must and for me this holy prayer begins my day. No one and nothing else can be so consistently relied upon to get me to this place, this center.

Gloria Logan

• EIGHTEEN

Get away from my desk
please
Go find you own space
please
No I won't be a kool-aid mom
clean the oven and the fridge
and give a shit about
twenty teenagers
think about dinner (and make it)
sit in the sun with
little girls just up from their naps
and listen to their dreams
and worry about my undone homework
while you do your paper
at my desk
why do I need to say NO
in an explosion of
martyrdom
because I don't know how
to say yes to me yet in a
regular, sustained way
but I'm getting there.

Marsha Campbell

• NINETEEN

Exile—not from a country but from your
innermost core.
To wonder who you are apart from someone,
or will you disappear.
To fear being lost or are you already lost.
This is certainly the "Darkest Night of my Soul."
The pain at the bottom of that ever-moving
spiral—but is it the bottom? You only know
after you have begun to spiral up. Nothing
dramatic will happen—merely a change in view—
knowing you are coming home, home to yourself.

Vivian Barondes

• TWENTY

Milo was his name. He valued me, needed me, treasured me,
read to me, fought for me—can you imagine, fought for me—
even took me to be his sacred daughter and legally adopted me.

I loved his mind, his very being. Naturally I would follow
in his path so I studied journalism. How natural it felt
that I, too, would one day become Chief-of-Staff of the
Associated Press, speak seven languages, play the violin—
become like him: as filled and fulfilled and giving.

He was magical and still is. His very being, even after
his death, is my force. How extraordinary that I knew him
only a year and a half.

Jeanne Gayler

He's strong, thin, lithe, dark, and bearded—he hides in his beard!
But what's inside comes out through his intensely burning dark eyes:
his wisdom, insightfulness, brilliance.

Is it wisdom, or is it rather his know-it-all attitude, which always scares
me? It makes me back off, withdraw into safe, private, feminine ground.

Better be a good cook and mother, better scrub that dirty floor than
allow that dark creature within to make his foray out into the sunlight,
where he often gets me into trouble.

Rhea Kahn

TWENTY-ONE

Spring

It is a feeling that swells
within me as though from
the womb. Warm, moist, pulsating
with my own rebirth.
Needing no parental life seeds.

It gushes forth as a spring
from an unknown source.

It races over the rocks, glitters
in the sun and babbles with creation.

Miriam Phoebe Newton

I've been depressed over some winters,
but during the last couple I've settled
into the quietness, somber tones, early
darkness and found peace and beauty here.
    Now when I see the first crocus
peeping its head out I resist. I'm not
ready for spring. I resent all these brightly
blooming daffodils.
    Spring's born for me like a baby—
once begun it comes on fast and furious
and there's no stopping now and hardly
time to catch a breath.

Gloria Logan

Spring dances across the stage claiming, "My turn." "My time."
"I've waited in the wings, I've prepared my inner core, I've held my
mystery and now it's my moment!" "Watch me perform." "Watch my
wonder, look at my color." "I'll thrill you. Just stand and watch!"

Jeanne Gayler

• TWENTY-TWO

At some point every spring there is an instant when there is a smell in the air at a certain place—a smell not like anything else I know. I can't name it, maybe because it is the combination of everything at that particular place and that moment. Or maybe it is the earth calling with its symphony of the senses. And it is then that it is time to get out in my garden. Time to put on my oldest clothes, and oldest shoes and time to put my hair back. It is time to put my hands in the dirt. My mother the earth is calling. I am renewed.

Vivian Barondes

Heaven

My heaven is a place of tranquility; a place where I can refresh my mind, rejuvenate my body, and renew my spirit so that the day-to-day absurdities of life become bearable and even accepted as part of living. My home is a holy place because I can touch heaven there. I love to see the bright sun streaming through the windows; I love to hear the cool, clean water flowing in our aquarium; I love to watch the birds and the squirrels just outside my kitchen window feasting on sunflower seeds; I love my gardens, where I have tilled and toiled for the past twelve years.

But something has happened to my holy place. It's been invaded by little men. Little men who think of me as Mama. They follow me around, expect me to play with them, fix their meals, do their laundry, clean their noses, dry their tears, hold them, protect them. All of which I do . . .

It is no longer easy to hold a quiet conversation with my husband. It is no longer easy to even finish a thought. and for a while, it was not easy to touch Heaven around my home. There is evidence in every room and even in my gardens of little men invasions. But I've come to realize that my two little boys are part of my heaven now. I share it with them—and with their trucks in the garden, their balls in the goldfish pond, their socks under the table.

Brenda Tuttle

• TWENTY-THREE

The reason I'm such a goddam pleaser is because
it is hell for me to be in a place with people
where they are displeased with me or mad at me.
I can't stand being a disappointer. It is hell
for me to be abandoned emotionally by people I
love. I know this grows directly out of my
experience of my mother's death. But I'm learning
to live in hell and face my damnation directly.
Because the price I pay by having to be everything
for everybody else is too dear. Yet it is such
a struggle for me. And always will be.

Gloria Logan

My Version of Hell

In my private Hell, everyone has turned their backs on me—
or worse, they sit stone-faced in a circle, then turn and whisper "sweet
everythings" in each other's ears.

In daily moments, Hell wears the face of my teenage children, when
they ignore me or answer my earnest questions with bitter sarcasm—
as if to say, "Who are *you* to want to be a part of my life?"

It wears the face of my lover—or rather, his absence, the *lack* of his
face—when I am needing and wanting affirmation that I am not alone.

In my private Hell, death is Nothing, does not frighten me wearing
its bony white mask. It is rather the sense that no one is there for me.
Everyone is in love with everyone else, and I alone am isolated,
separated by a thick black veil.

Carolyn Cottom

TWENTY-FOUR

What If

What if we were really tolerant of differences—
    different religions, values, languages, and cultural practices?
What is we stood together and said NO to those who would take away
    the rights of others?
What if all children were viewed as our own children, so that no child
    was allowed to be hungry, or homeless, uneducated or without
    health care?
What if we insisted that time and space be made for family life;
    time for caring for our elderly; for spending time together; time for
    meeting child and health care needs without financial devastation?
What would happen if we placed greater value on people's actions than
    on their possessions or positions of power?
What if to live simply was applauded?
What if we valued accomplishment in the home or personal relation-
    ships as much as we value accomplishments in the world or work?
What if we supported artists so their visions could be shared more
    widely?
What if we encouraged creativity in everyone?

Eloise Singh

We're making progress in our family.
Women are already in the temple.
They are writing hymnals,
Singing the sacred songs
and sitting at the head table with the VIPs.

Our gatekeeper opens the door for everyone to come in.
We've an easy access ramp for the handicapped,
Child-sized furniture for the children,
There are roles for everyone in the passion play.

Some men are afraid and stand outside in the rain.
Sullen and afraid to COME IN
They PEEK IN at the windows
Mock the services as trivial
The architecture as derivative.

They are hungry and we wish to share bread.
They are thirsty and we have holy water.

Come and take communion with us, in peace.
Let this earth be a house for ALL.
WELCOME HOME.

Joan Starr

• TWENTY-FIVE

Prior to my job interview I went to the Louisville equivalent of
Woodies and paid a modest $250 for an interview suit. I paid another
$50 for a pair of black Joyce pumps. My hair was cut at one of the most
prestigious hairstylist's. I interviewed for the job as a staff attorney and
was hired.

Now I have torn the shoulder pads out of the jacket. I do not wear
the black herring-bone A-line skirt, and the black Joyce pumps sit in the
closet, gathering dust. The women who ride the elevator in my office
building all wear varying degrees of the professional garb. I particularly
notice the shoes—a different pump for every pompadour.

The pump—that vicious little animal that bites women's toes and
keeps them off balance all day—ankles swollen and hurting in the
evening. Men should have to wear them for a year. The pump is for
western wear the equivalent of the Chinese binding of feet. What if we
all let our feet spread out to their full stature? My friend wears size 9-D
sandals—would that my feet will grow to that size!

Rose Ashcraft

I am increasingly uncomfortable in suits. I don my suit of armor and
become a gladiator, too often orating a position that I do not agree with.
I think of yesterday of my cross-examination of a woman with bi-polar
disorder. Does the national security require that she lose her security
clearance and her job? Am I complicit? I don my suit. I stand behind the
podium. I play this role for five hours without even being allowed a
break for lunch. After it's over, a friend who observed does not con-
gratulate me on my performance; she feels sorry for the woman who
looked defensive under my cross-examination. I go home and take off
the suit.

Kathy Braeman

• TWENTY-SIX

For OLYMPIA BROWN
(first American woman denominationally ordained
into the ministry, by the Universalists, in 1863)

Today I begin your biography
early. It's snowing, though
spring. I relive this season
in Europe, awaiting acceptance
by your Antioch. In the
snow rain sleet hail
of that spring there was only
one truth: your trinity of womanhood
going to army wives' teas.

This week's rain drips from tree
branches, flows over lawns, down
gutters, gurgles under the streets,
tributary streams of your second trinity:
EXPERIENCE INSTRUCTION INSPIRATION
for you becoming one in the ministry.
I struggle through seasons of fear
that the "unseen" within be forever forsaken.

New blossoms bloat on the tree limbs
and still it is snowing. This is
the feminine season: moisture puddles
in this field of time. Sleet starts again
and the sacred heads wounded are
those of the earliest daffodils.

GCR

Harriet Tubman

   I feel like I could write her story,
because I have felt like a spy and an underground
guerrilla in this man's world. I am, like her,
a survivor of a kind of slavery. And we walked
at night feeling our way through the darkness—led
by moss growing on the north side of trees
and the light of our faith in that which is Divine.
Moss and trees, darkness and hope and the courage
of a few who dared to help.

Marsha Campbell

• TWENTY-SEVEN

In the beginning there was darkness, and chaos, and Mind.
Mind wandered about in the darkness, bumping into Chaos,
stumbling over and around Chaos until there was nothing left
to do but put Chaos in order. In the process of organizing
Chaos, Mind would once in a while catch a glimpse of a small
brightness in the Dark. Gradually, little by little, the brightness
became focused into a spark. The spark became clearer,
and brighter and became Spirit, who joined Mind in organizing Chaos.
    Spirit and Mind wandered on through the Dark until they felt
themselves more joined together in their search. They built themselves a
protective coating—a body—they put on arms and legs—they became
Person—Mind/Spirit/Body.
    Person multiplied and became fruitful and Spirit became Universal
Consciousness. Mind became all the Sciences and Organizations. All are
still careful to guard unconditional Love which is the basic force of all
Life.

Ada Churchill

I am the face of the deep which darkness falls upon.
I split and from my being springs the light but it
is not such a big deal. For I spring up light in
sweet and sprightly ways. I don't exude. I bubble.
I giggle forth happy children of light. And they dance
and they eat and they tire and nestle closely together
and I feel their breath on my endless neck. They dig
into me with their hands and form little pockets of light
in my darkness. They hide in me and I push them back out
into the light. Sometimes they cry because it is too bright.
I receive them always.

Beth Hudson Latture

• TWENTY-EIGHT

The Sacred

Being rocked in a mother's arms.
Being loved beyond anything.
Feeling peace at being connected.
The sacred is the quiet place.
The deepest place. The most loving place.

Gloria Logan

Image of the Sacred

ONE is the name with the power
to make sacred special places
when full of holy energy the hands
transmute the dross into gold,
the light into dark
the dark into rainbow
the nightmare into paradise
One plays with the colors, smell and taste
bringing all into orbit
dancing from ring to ring.

Joan Starr

• TWENTY-NINE

I AM like the iceberg. Only a small part visible to the eye. But so much more to give that is not so easily seen by others or by myself.

And I am a gazelle who will glide through with grace, moving forward through the risks, pain, and disappointments; and hoping to catch some joy and peace on the way.

Since knowing that in some Mid-Eastern languages grace and rain mean the same, it is easier to accept that *both* are necessary to continue the journey.

Vivian Barondes

I AM the searcher. Looking for connections. Waiting to be joined with everything—with Light and Dark, hope, despair, people, rocks, Emotions, logic—I want to find it all, connect to every bit of it.

I come from a place of restraint where all feelings are muffled, all joy is suspect. A place of passivity, depression and unavailable emotions.

I am a butterfly—I am a soul—searching for that stage in my metamorphosis where I will know light, hope, how to be assertive, and compassionate.

I am a rainbow, the bridge across which goddesses walk searching for souls. That wonderful scarf of color that reassures us the storm is over—serenity is here for a while.

I, the searcher, am coming home. Home to a place I have not found—a place of understanding, respect, stress, guilt: all the old feelings come with me. But when I am home, I can sort them out and have control over what is to be done with them. I will be master of that butterfly that flutters within: my soul. I follow the Cosmic spirit which lifts me stage by stage to wider spaces.

Ada Churchill

• THIRTY

Flowering

Awakening to an early spring snow fearing winter can again regain its hold, the budding forsythia again become sticks on which to hang eggs red from other crushed springs, shared instinct says NO! The cultivated forsythia's been with us so long it mirrors our human behavior: inner sparks, once started, become little bursts of the sun, shaped like the stars we all come from. Though some have been burned by the cold, bruised by snow, spring's message is not of a martyred dying but of the will to survive, bearing witness to life; and with the forsythia, we find ourselves flowering with hope.

Flowering

Awakening to an early spring
snow fearing winter can regain

its hold, the budding forsythia
again become sticks on which

to hang eggs red from other
crushed springs, shared instinct

says NO! The cultivated forsythia's
been with us so long it mirrors

our human behavior: inner sparks,
once started, become little

bursts of the sun, shaped like
the stars we all come from. Though

some have been burned by the cold,
bruised by snow, spring's message

is not of a martyred dying
but of the will to survive, bearing

witness to life; and with the forsythia,
we find ourselves flowering with hope.

GCR

WORKING BIBLIOGRAPHY

Realizing that the insights and information I've used out of context are subject to misinterpretation, I enclose a list of the books that have informed my thinking as I developed the writing exercises for this project. Many of the books have been cited in the text. I encourage you to delve into the original material, let it speak to and through your life, and perhaps even suggest other writings for you to do. But mostly, enjoy!

Barth, Edna. *Lilies, Rabbits, and Painted Eggs, The Story of the Easter Symbols*. New York: Clarion Books, 1970.

Bennett, Anne McGrew. *From Woman-Pain to Woman-Vision*. Ed. Mary E. Hunt. Minneapolis: Fortress Press, 1989.

Bolen, Jean Shinoda. *Goddesses In Everywoman*. New York: Harper and Row, 1984.

Boulding, Elise. *The Underside of History*, A View of Women Through Time. Boulder: Westview Press, 1976.

Campbell, Joseph. *The Inner Reaches of Outer Space, Metaphor As Myth and As Religion*. New York: Alfred Van Der Marck, 1985.

_____. *Myths To Live By*. New York: Bantam, 1972.

Christ, Carol. *Diving Deep and Surfacing, Women Writers on Spiritual Quest*. Boston: Beacon Press, 1980.

_____ and Judith Plaskow, Ed. *Womanspirit Rising*. San Francisco: Harper and Row, 1979.

Cooney, Robert and Helen Michalowski, Ed. *The Power of the People, Active Nonviolence in the United States*. Philadelphia: New Society Publishers, 1987.

de Castillejo, Irene Claremont. *Knowing Woman*. New York: Harper and Row, 1982.

Gilligan, Carol. *In A Different Voice*. Cambridge: Harvard University Press, 1982.

Harding, M. Ester. *Woman's Mysteries*. New York: Bantam, 1973.

Morton, Nelle. *The Journey Is Home*. Boston: Beacon Press, 1985.

Mumford, Lewis. *The Myth of the Machine*. New York: Harcourt, Brace and World, Inc., 1962.

Ostriker, Alicia Suskin. *Stealing the Language*. Boston: Beacon Press, 1986.

Pratt, Annis. *Archetypal Patterns in Women's Fiction*. Bloomington: Indiana University Press, 1981.

Sanford, John A. *The Invisible Partners*. New York: Paulist Press, 1980.

Sarton, May. *Writings On Writing*. Maine: Puckerbrush Press, 1980.

Walker, Barbara G. *The Woman's Dictionary of Symbols & Sacred Objects*. San Francisco: Harper and Row, 1988.

Woolf, Virginia. *A Room of One's Own*. St. Albans: Triad/Panther Books, 1977.

_____. *Three Guineas*. New York: Harcourt Brace Jovanovich, Inc., 1966.

Gail Ranadive was born in Boston, Massachusetts,
and graduated from Lawrence General Hospital
School of Nursing. She has an M.A. in Peace Studies
from Antioch, and an M.F.A. in Creative Writing
from The American University, where she's taught
composition and creative writing. She's also taught at
Georgetown University and at the Writer's Center in
Bethesda, Maryland. She's been writer-in-residence at
St. Mary's College Festival of Poetry, and a Fellow at
the Virginia Center for the Creative Arts. Her poetry
has been published nationally. She currently lives
with her husband outside of Washington, D.C. They
have two grown daughters.